handwriting

Shirley Clarke & Barry Silsby

Illustrated by Tony Wells

BROCKHAMPTON PRESS
LONDON

NOTES FOR PARENTS

Research has shown that when children and parents work together at home, the child's work at school improves.

The purpose of the *Headstart* books is to provide activities which your child will enjoy doing and which will encourage learning to take place in the home.

Each of the activities in this book is designed to help your child develop good handwriting habits.

You can help your child get the most out of this book by:

- *giving help* where necessary (for example, by reading instructions);
- *reading the advice below.* This gives further information and explains the purpose of each activity;
- *talking* to your child about an activity, to encourage him or her;
- *showing enthusiasm* and interest in your child's involvement in the book. (Confidence grows with adult approval.)

It is important to encourage good writing habits from the start, but it is also important for your child to be relaxed. You should check the following:

Grip   If your child has problems with the grip, get him or her to pinch the thumb and forefinger together like a crab. The pen or pencil should be gripped between these two digits and rested on the middle finger in any way that is comfortable. The pen or pencil should be in the crease between the thumb and forefinger.

Posture   It is best for your child to sit at a table when writing, but most adult tables are too high for them to write at comfortably. Some suggestions for overcoming this are shown on page 4.

Left or right-handed?   Your child should be naturally left or right-handed. Left-handed children need to develop different writing strategies from right-handed children, as shown on page 5.

6–7 It's raining, it's pouring

This pattern helps your child to maintain a parallel writing style, as well as helping with the formation of the letters b h i j k l m n p r t.

8–9 Clowning around

This helps your child with the letters h m n r.

10–11 Perky pelicans

This shape helps your child with joining writing, as well as with the letters i l u y.

12–13 Never smile at a crocodile

This pattern helps with the letters v w x.

14–15 Ogling owls

This pattern helps with the formation of the letters a c d g o q and prepares your child for pages 16–17.

16–17 Silly snakes

This is the beginning of the most difficult pattern which is seen in full on pages 20–21. It helps with joining, as well as with the letters a c d e g o q s.

18–19 Wise owls

This pattern helps with horizontal joins, as well as with the letters a c d e g o q.

20–21 More silly snakes

This pattern is difficult and your child might need to practise page 20 several times before progressing to page 21. It helps with joining writing and the letters a c d e g o q s.

22–23 24 Dinosaur backs

All of the patterns in this book are revised on these pages.

THINGS TO REMEMBER

You can hold your pen or pencil with two or three fingers like this.

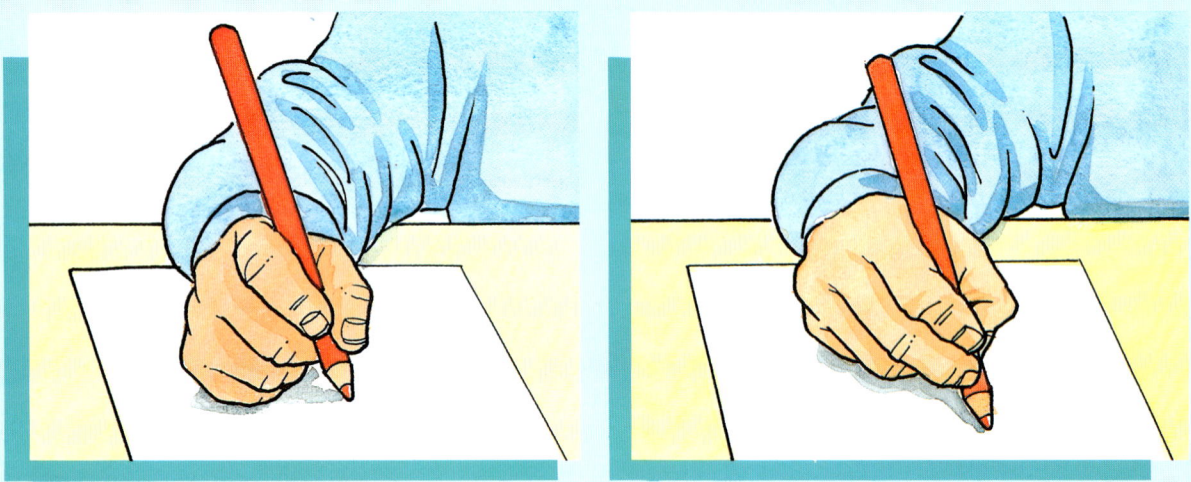

Grip your pen or pencil just above the part where it begins to go into a point.

If you sit at a full-sized table to write, you might find it uncomfortable. Try making yourself higher by sitting on a stool or putting a cushion on your chair.

If you write with your right hand, you should sit like this.

The top of your pen or pencil should be pointing over your right shoulder. Your right elbow should be by your side with your left hand holding the book.

If you write with your left hand, you should sit like this.

The top of your pen or pencil should be pointing over your left shoulder. Your left elbow should be by your side with your right hand holding the book.

It's raining, it's pouring

The artist has forgotten to put the rain in this picture. Can you put it in for her? Put in as much rain as you like.
Start at the top of the raindrop and move your pen or pencil down like this

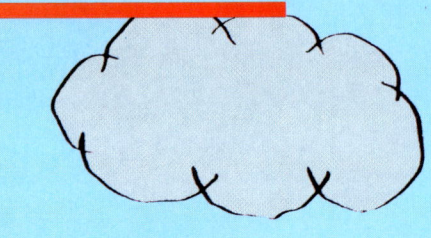

Now try some of these patterns. Start at the • and move your pen or pencil down, just like with the raindrops.

Clowning around

These clowns have forgotten to paint their eyebrows. Can you draw them in?

Start on the ∨ and try to do each eyebrow without stopping.

Can you draw the shape without a clown? Try here.

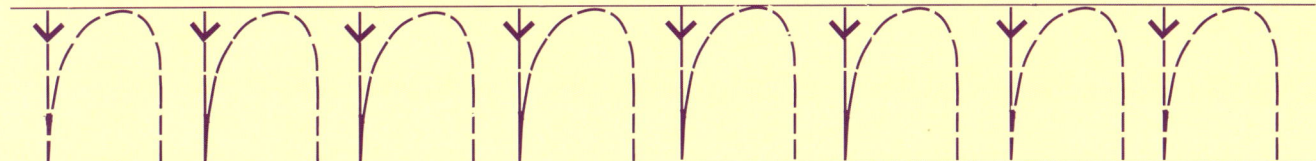

These shapes are joined together. Can you write all the way to the end without taking your pencil off the page? Go over the lines to start with and finish on your own.

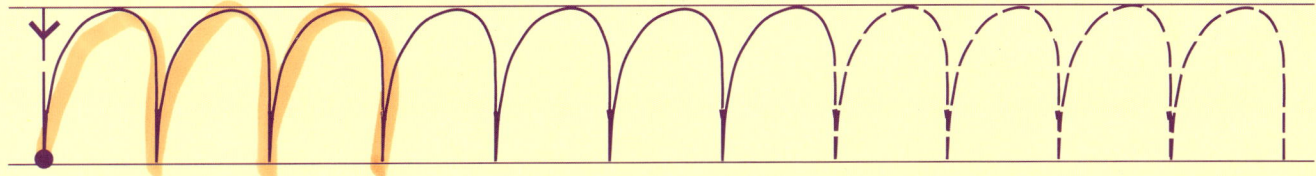

Try these yourself.

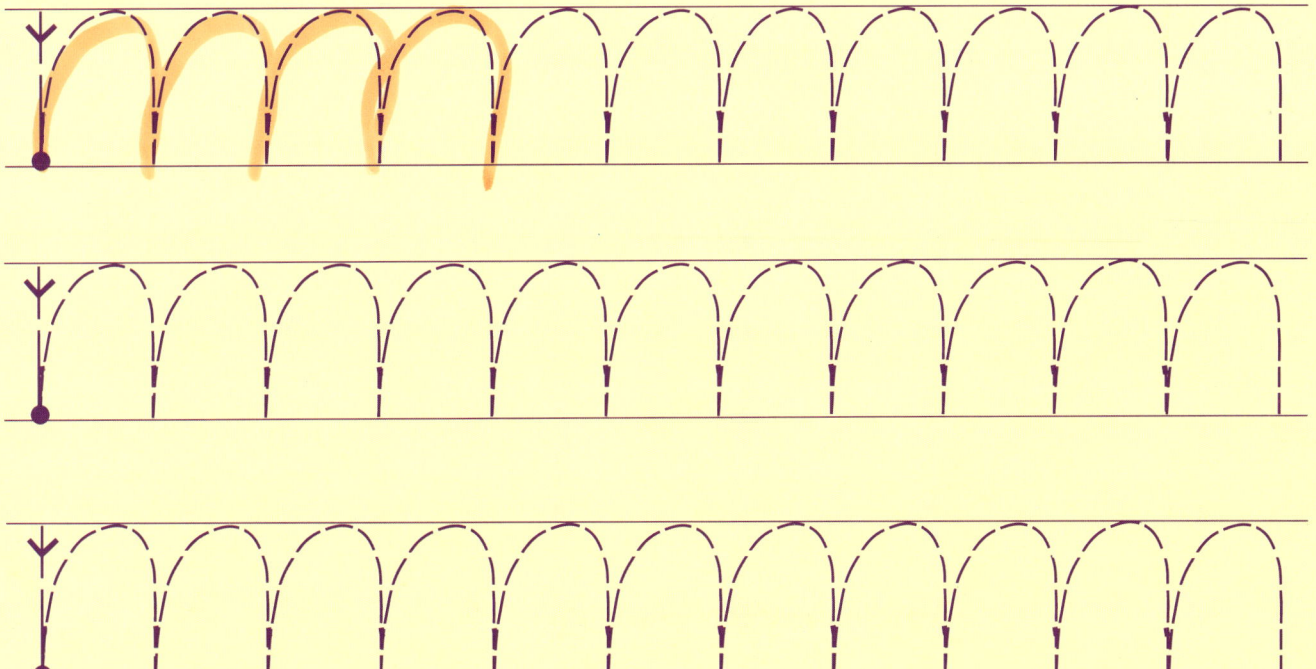

9

Can you join up lots of pelican shapes like this?

Try these yourself.

Never smile at a crocodile

Draw in the crocodile's teeth and the ridges on her back. Can you also finish the mountains in the background?

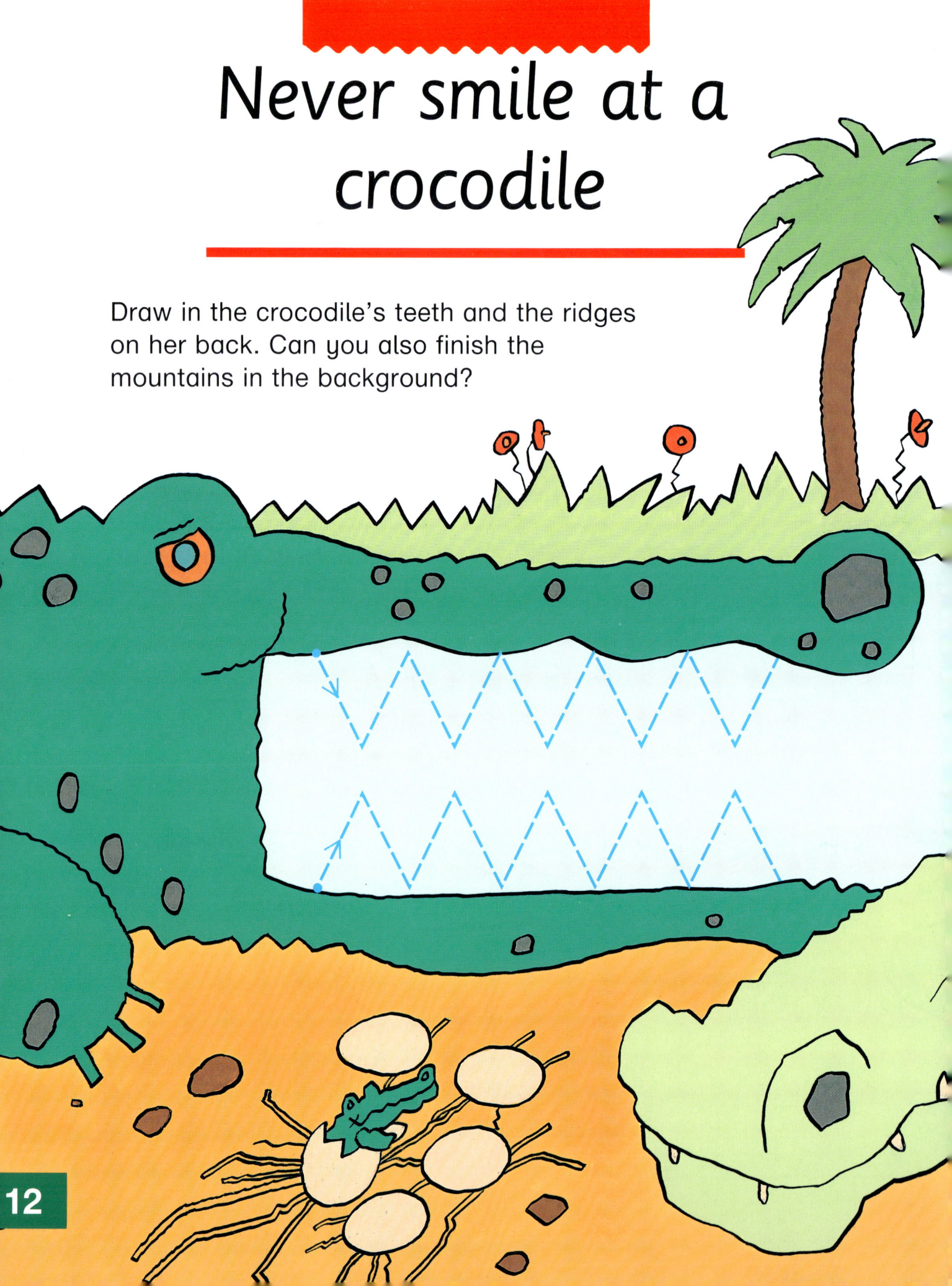

Now try these shapes without the owls.

Try these on your own. Think carefully where to start and which way to move your pen or pencil.

Silly snakes

Silly snakes are always looking at their tails!

Can you draw a line from their nose to the tip of their tail?

Remember to keep your pencil point inside the snake's body.

Can you draw a snake shape?
Start at the dot and try to stay on the line.

Wise owls

Wise owls wear special glasses.

Can you draw their shape?

Start on the ↖• and go all the way around. Don't stop. When you reach the • again, go across to the ○ and follow the arrow all the way around. Try lots of times with different colours.

More silly snakes

Do you remember the silly snakes on page 16? This silly snake has put his tail on another snake's head. Try to draw a line from the first snake's nose to the third snake's tail **without stopping**.

Now try these.

When these shapes are joined up, they look like waves on the sea. Draw the sea in these pictures. Do each one without stopping. Make sure you touch each •.

Dinosaur backs

These dinosaurs have all sorts of shapes on their backs.
Draw in the shapes for them.
Can you see any other shapes to fill in?

Now try them for yourself on plain paper.

British Library Cataloguing in Publication Data
Clarke, Shirley
  Headstart: handwriting. – (Help your child)
  I. Title II. Silsby, Barry III. Series
  372.6

ISBN 1-86019-517-2

First published 1991
Second impression 1992
This edition published 1997 by Brockhampton Press, a member of Hodder Headline PLC Group.
10 9 8 7 6 5 4 3
1999 1998 1997

© 1991 Shirley Clarke and Barry Silsby

All rights reserved. No part of this publication may be reproduced or transmitted in any form or by any means, electronic or mechanical, including photocopy, recording, or any information storage and retrieval system, without permission in writing from the publisher or under licence from the Copyright Licensing Agency Limited. Further details of such licences (for reprographic reproduction) may be obtained from the Copyright Licensing Agency Limited, of 90 Tottenham Court Road, London WIP 9HE.

Typeset by Oxprint, Oxford OX2 6TR.

Printed in India.